Secrets of Supply Chain Management

By

ANDREI BESEDIN

<u>www.wiseexcel.com</u>

Copyright © 2018

TABLE OF CONTENTS

LEGAL NOTES AND DISCLAIMER

Text Copyright © [ANDREI BESEDIN]

Legal & Disclaimer

CHAPTER 1. MAKING IT REAL

With supply chain effectiveness and efficiency so tightly bound to the success of a company, it's surprising that so many companies have no defined Supply Chain Strategy. However, defining a strategy is just the first step. The Supply Chain Strategy has to be right, and it has to be followed by the right actions.

One company's strategy is unlikely to be the same as another companies, even if they have overlapping business goals. The strategy has to be defined both regarding the market that the company wants to address and the business strategy that it has formulated as a function of its business objectives.

The indispensable starting point is what the customer values.This, in turn, drives the company's business objectives. Different market segments may be focused on offerings that are continually being renewed, on service and quality, or on low prices. The retailing market abounds with examples.Fashion retailers such as Zara and H&M have focused their business strategy on short life cycle products.Their Supply Chain Strategy has to fit with this as well as with their corporate objectives. Supermarket chains like Tesco and Wal-Mart need very low cost and efficient supply chains to compete effectively. Solutions focused retailers such as Home Depot will have a focus on elements such as buying well, maintaining high availability and proper range management.

Supply Chain Strategy is just one part of a company's overall business strategy, albeit a key part. What often confuses companies is that whereas an overall Supply Chain Strategy must be defined and linked to the business strategy, it often also needs to be adapted to individual divisions within the company.

Focusing on the End Game – the Results Required

Successful businesses are centered on what their customers want. Their Supply Chain Strategy follows the same rule.There's an extra twist, however, because supplying customers with what they want is also dependent on what value they expect and where they are located. A company like Tesco has its points of presence in towns and similar metro areas. Their customers come to these points of presence, meaning the Tesco stores. The company focus is on availability, price, and range. Compare that with another company serving the mining sector with products and services as diverse as explosives, surveys and drilling, and customers remotely and widely dispersed. In this case, service is critical, but the cost may not be so sensitive. And somewhere between them are pharmaceutical retailers, like boots where cost is still a factor but where the products can absorb a little more of the cost and customers value a higher level of service.

Examples of "end game" parameters for different companies include:

Your End Game?	Always in Stock	Lowest Prices	Quality Products
Enablers Systems & Infrastructure	DC Network Fleet WMS Replen Systems		
Enablers People & Process	Structure Capability & Skills Change Management Plans Communication process Measures (KPIs)		

Healthcare:

Service assurance, best compliance, best range

Building Products:

Delivery where you want, all your products in one place, the price is never an issue.

3PL (3rd Party Logistics):

Best service reliability, best sector knowledge, no unhappy customers.

Mass Retailer:

Always in stock, lowest prices, quality products

Supply chains often encompass a broad range of business and customer needs. Companies need to be able to see beyond the complexity to identify the things that matter. This is what then determines the key functions and processes to be focused on. At the customer end, what often matters is service and availability. Within the business itself, the cost of goods sold is the key parameter.

The operational decisions come afterward as a result of how the Supply Chain Strategy has been defined. Specific IT systems and decisions about whether to outsource are the "how" in the process and must necessarily be preceded by the "what." Good Supply Chain Strategy focuses on the end game; good operational management takes care of the details.

There are still trade-offs to be made, even within the context of maintaining the overall strategic direction for the supply chain. Strategic thinking has to be continually present, or trade-offs can lead to isolationist ("silo") thinking and suboptimal implementations. Getting the trade-offs wrong in a physical distribution network, for example regarding the number of stocking locations, the products to be held and the service to be provided to customers, can account for as much as 15% of distribution costs.

When strategic imperatives are clearly defined and respected, your company is protected against the muddled thinking that can occur where, for example, distribution centers (DCs) are outsourced as a matter of policy (without considering what suits the business best) or where transport assets are kept in-house regardless of supply chain effectiveness and cost.

The value streams associated with the supply chain give another useful perspective and a way of ensuring that the supply chain, when implemented, will fit with business strategy and customer expectations. The diverse range of customers and products that exist in the healthcare sector makes a good example. We can use categories as follows: continuity products with a year-round pull; non-continuity products with a magnetic pipeline pull; and seasonal products with push, pull and exit. Then if, for example, our strategic imperative is low cost to the end customer, supply chain costs have to be minimized. This starts with buying, not only the starting point for the supply chain but also typically one of its highest costs.

Getting Buy-In Across the Business

Managing all these functions and processes effectively needs good information visibility, good cross-functional communications, and everyone knowing what the end game is. We now have our strategic imperatives, and they drive our tactics, our plans, our resourcing and ultimately our results. But we need to constantly balance and adjust our tactics to keep targeting these imperatives.

Establishing the strategic imperatives for your business is a critical stage in developing an effective Supply Chain Strategy or, where one already exists, in ensuring it's effective. The strategic imperatives relate directly to the overall business objectives and for this reason must be developed at the highest level of the organization. Optimally, this means senior management participants from all key areas of the business and most importantly the CEO. It needs not be a lengthy or time-consuming process, but this level of engagement is essential. The senior management team needs to be actively involved in the process of translating the business objectives to supply chain objectives, because the Supply Chain Strategy, once developed, will impact them all.

The objective here is to get all department heads on the same page regarding what the supply chain is trying to do. Depending on the level of supply chain understanding in the business, this may require some education regarding the cost-benefit implications regarding key supply decisions. To assist the process, it's best to demonstrate the benefits of various supply chain objectives to other functions within the business. For example:

Sales: Highlight how the strategy will focus on improved availability and sales.

Merchandising: Highlight how the strategy will focus on reduced markdowns, improved sell-through, and improved overall margins.

All key functions in the business need to understand the WIIFM (What's In It for me), regarding the business overall and all key functional areas. Once,the senior management team, is engaged and has agreed the Supply Chain Strategy at a conceptual level, work can begin on greater levels of detail and engaging lower levels of management in the business.

It's still vitally important that,at all levels of the business, the strategic imperatives are embraced, as they should shape the plans and actions of all within the supply chain. The strategy must also be seen to be driven from the top. We need to be conscious, however, that as we work at the lower levels of the organization, priorities, and viewpoints will change. This is largely driven by the managers' areas of responsibility and reward structure.

In most cases, it will be necessary to adapt and build on the strategy, to give it a more tactical and operational interpretation. It's then also important to start changing key performance indicators (KPIs) and reward structures, where these may conflict with the strategy. It's also important, at all levels of the organization, that the Supply Chain Strategy and, in particular, the strategic imperatives are seen as the end game. They are the overall objectives that must constantly be strived for. The means to the ends, the various tactics, and operational plans may change over time. In fact, they usually will, as the shape and needs of the business change. The trick is to ensure that the tactical and operational plans do not become end games in themselves.

Measuring Results Effectively

At the top level, measure the end game. At lower levels, measure the operational effectiveness. Measurements is made using KPIs. For example, top-level goals concerning cost and service will then cascade down to level 2 and level 3 KPIs. Cost may be expressed as supply chain dollars as a percentage of sales. From this, we could have DC dollars as a percentage of sales and then DC direct dollars per unit and DC total dollars per unit. Naturally, the specific KPIs to be used will be heavily influenced by the specific industry and business under consideration. Like the strategic imperatives, ample opportunity must be allowed for key stakeholders to engage in the process of developing the KPI matrix.

S.I.	Service				Cost				
L1	On Shelf Availability				Supply Chain $ as % Sales				
L2	Store OSA	DC Availability	SIFOT	DIFOT	DC $ as % Sales	Sec Tpt $ as % of Sales	Prim Tpt as % of Sales	COGS as % of Sales	Inv $ at Cost
				Level 3 Example					
L3	DC Units / Direct Hr	DC Direct $ per Unit	DC Total $ per Unit	Total Direct Supply Units	Total DC Units	Total DC Hours	Forecast Vol v Actual Vol	Lost Time	Labour Retention

The key to measuring supply chain results is that KPIs have to be directly linked to the supply chain strategic imperatives. If not, people will be motivated to achieve the wrong things. To establish the strategic imperatives first and then determine the KPIs that will have the greatest impact on supporting them. At lower levels in the organization, additional operational KPIs will appear, and this is fair and reasonable to allow managers to measure the performance of key functional areas, but they must not conflict with the strategic imperatives.

Perils and Pitfalls That You Can Avoid

In the light of what we have discussed so far, it's not hard to see where supply chain strategies might go wrong. Typical issues include:

• Failure to appreciate the end game. This occurs when the Supply Chain Strategy is developed in isolation and does not take into account the strategic objectives of the business.

• Failure to understand customer needs. This can result in under or over servicing with a negative impact on service and costs.

• Over-estimating competencies. Sometimes the competencies of existing staff and systems can create major hurdles for strategy success. If in doubt, simplify down the strategy and take basic steps first.

• Failure to get senior management commitment. This is probably the major cause for failure and will occur if the senior management team has not been engaged in developing the strategy. If it has not been involved, the strategy may also simply be wrong.

• Failure to get employee commitment. Any new strategy needs to be seen to be driven from the top.It also needs to be translated into the tactical and operational language of others within the business.

• Poor change management. Many companies will try to impose a strategy on employees, whereas the greatest chance of success is supported by a high degree of engagement, communication,and training at all levels of the organization.

• Poor communication. Poor communication not only occurs internally within businesses, but changes in strategy need to be well communicated with suppliers and customers alike.

Companies That Get It Right
Nokia India – significant success in India
Mobile phone manufacturer Nokia has used its supply chain to forge significant success in India, with an effective and innovative Supply Chain Strategy developed to support aggressive business targets. They have manufacturing in Chennai, with R&D in Bangalore, Hyderabad, and Mumbai. India has very high mobile phone usage, probably because mobile tariffs are some of the lowest in the world. Mobile phone usage increased from about 1% - 8% in about five years. The agricultural market potential in India is huge, with a telephone density as little as one-tenth of that of urban areas.

In India, Nokia has invested heavily at the lower end of the market, even specifically designing much cheaper phones. In India, most phones are sold by retailers, not the mobile phone companies, and there are about 100,000 retail outlets. Nokia has used the services of HCL as their distribution partner to reach all the small towns nationally. HCL already had a significant distribution network for their products. Nokia even uses a mobile van marketing program to take the mobile phone message to the small country villages.

H&M – fashion at reasonable prices

H&M is the world's third-largest retailer, with 1,600 stores in 33 countries. Their focus is fashion at reasonable prices.

They have 20 production offices in Asia and Europe and have about 800 suppliers.Their key to success is a well-integrated supply chain. The Stockholm HQ designs the clothes, which are then made in Asia and Europe; Europe for the faster turnaround products and Asia for the long lead time products. Store replenishment is an extreme focus to ensure high levels of availability. The supply chain is managed from the HQ, and H&M acts as an importer, wholesaler, and retailer. H&M manage the stock with a DC in each country, but transport is outsourced. This is a good example of a well-developed Supply Chain Strategy effectively supporting the business goals.

A Simple Roadmap for Developing or Realigning a Supply Chain Strategy
We can certainly learn a lot from some of these best in class companies, but we must be careful not to just overlay their strategies on our own companies. We need to examine and select the appropriate elements and adapt those for our use. What is appropriate for one continent may not be for another one. Australia, for example, has a similar surface area to Europe. However, marked differences exist for physical distribution regarding customer density, sales density, replenishment times and sourcing points, to name a few. Adopting supply chain strategies without adaptation is unwise, but it's certainly possible to learn from them.

CHAPTER 2. CUSTOMER SERVICE

It really does all start here – with the customer, and the service that is provided to them. And, it ends here as well since successful organizations have one central focus – customer service excellence. Many preach this mantra that 'the customer is king' or other similar themes but, in the words of Shakespeare, this touted focus is 'more honored in the breach than the observance.'

This chapter will address an approach to customer service based on the supply chain's pivotal and critical role in delivering and assisting the business with delivering:

a)   Customer Service Excellence, and

b)   Customer Loyalty.

While intrinsically linked, each of these will be dealt with separately since, from a supply chain and indeed whole of business perspective, the measurement systems used for each are, or ought to be, different.

CUSTOMER SERVICE EXCELLENCE

There are many views about customer service excellence, what a customer expects, what is valued by customers and what is not, the role of the supply chain and what kind of

Measurement systems best capture this information in a timely way to permit organizations to respond quickly. Since the operation of and service delivered by the supply chain in business has such an important part to play in the overall customer experience, it is appropriate to ask the question, "Is there an ultimate measure of customer service?"

One measurement approach increasingly adopted by more and more businesses is the Perfect Order. The ultimate measure of customer service is the Perfect, or Error Free, Order. This measure requires that there are no mistakes across all six key functional areas of the supply chain that interact to provide the customer with what they expect:

- The Right Product.

- At the Right Time.

- In the Right Place.

- In the Right Quantity.

- At the Right Price.

The six components referred to are outlined as follows and are presented in chronological sequence from the point of order receipt and capture to a content delivery.

1. Order Entry Accuracy

Order entry accuracy or order capture is dependent on two factors. These are:

a)   Capturing the customer's first request.

   The first request is sometimes known as an unconstrained order, or in other words, what the customer wanted in the first instance without any constraints being placed on the order – for example, insufficient stock. This is a vital component of delivering customer service excellence yet is only adopted by a few organizations. Those that do are typically operating Best in Class supply chains. Why is capturing this so important? The answer lies in using this data point as a basis for forecasting future demand.In most organizations demand planning is based on historical sales – actual sales. In a very simplistic case to illustrate the point, if 100 units of an item were purchased of an SKU for each of the last three months, it is likely that 100 per month will be ordered for future months. If, in addition to the actual consumption of 100 units per month, over the preceding months there was an unfulfilled demand of another 100 units, then not only would the forecast not take this into account, but there would always be an insufficient stock to meet real or unconstrained demand. In this instance, the customer's perception, if this were perpetual, is that the supplying company could only ever supply 50% of what the customer wanted. And this would continue, unbroken based on this process, unless something dramatic changed.

This scenario too is premised on not being able to fill orders to the quantity required. The impact of product substitution has a far worse compounding effect on the level of service, cost of holding inventory and product obsolescence. This example might demonstrate the point. If 10 units of Product A constituted the customer's first request, but insufficient stock was available at the time of order placement, yet a negotiated order resulted in an equivalent number of units of Product B ordered instead as a substitute, then, unless corrected, forward demand planning would be based on consumption of 10 units of Product B. In the following month, 10 units of Product B would be procured to meet a supposed demand that was in fact fictitious. If the same customer called in the subsequent month and again wanted to place an order for ten units of Product A, the result would be:

- No stock of Product A that the customer wanted.

- An equivalent number of items of Product B for which there were no orders.

- Inflated inventory of Product B.

- Missed sales for Product A.

- The potential for product obsolescence of Product B.

- Poor forecast accuracy for both of these Store-Keeping Units (SKUs).

Delivering a Perfect or Error Free Order, therefore, depends, in the first instance, on having appropriate procedures in place to capture and utilize a customer's first request. For each order transmittal method – phone, fax and electronic – different processes are required to capture an unconstrained order properly.

b) On the basis that the above is in place, the next sequential step in delivering a Perfect Order is accurate to order entry, i.e., no data keying errors, no transpositional errors, etc. In an age of e-business and electronic transfer of orders, errors in this component of delivering a Perfect Order have been significantly reduced.

2. Inventory Availability

If a customer's order is captured based on their first request and accurately entered, to this point, the order remains in a perfect or error Free State.

The next requirement of a supply chain is to have sufficient stock to meet the captured demand. This is dependent on 2 factors:

a)   A level of forecast accuracy that predicted the demand ahead of time. A good forecasting system and process, perhaps including CPFR (Collaborative Planning Forecasting and Replenishment), can assist in delivering this outcome.

b)   Secondly, even if the forecast is accurate, the stock must physically be received into stock and be 'available for sale'. This metric then is also linked to supplier performance to ensure that the inventory is available at the time of order receipt. If the inventory is available then, again, to this point in the delivery of a Perfect Order, the process is without error and likely to deliver customer service excellence.

3 . Warehouse Performance

Ostensibly a warehouse or DC, in order to maintain the Perfect Order chain, needs to achieve the following:

• Pick the order without error, i.e. pick errors.

• Not sustain any damage to the product during the process.

- Complete all warehousing functions in time to meet the required despatch time that is linked to the customer lead time for delivery according to that which is promised.

4. Carrier Delivery On Time and In Full

Once the warehouse has completed all its functions, the onus to maintain an Error Free status passes to a nominated transport company in most cases. If they are able to deliver 100 percent on time and in full then the order retains its Perfect Order status.

5. Customer Acceptance of Order

If all of the above steps have been completed without failure or defect, and the delivery is completed not only on time, without shortages or loss and also without damage, then a customer might be reasonably expected to sign to acknowledge acceptance.

6. Invoice Accuracy

Given the above, if all have been completed then the physical delivery is perfect, and so what remains to complete the process, complete the order and conclude the transaction, is payment by the customer based on not only there being no service defects, but the invoice details are correct also. For example, the right price is applied; the invoice matches the goods delivered, correct product codes, etc.

So, based on the above, what is the probability of an order being perfect? The following benchmarking reporting format developed by Benchmarking Success demonstrates the calculated probability of a Perfect or Error Free Order for a sample and typical organization.

The Perfect (Error Free) Order

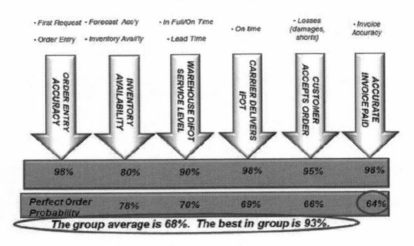

For this case study, the probability of a Perfect Order was 64%, compared with the average for the similar group of 68%. But what is even more revealing is that the best in the group was achieving 93%. For this organization, this became the customer service 'high bar' that they set about achieving.And this became a 'whole of business' focus.A monthly reporting cycle was established to measure the probability of a Perfect Order across the whole business, and this was used as the ultimate customer service excellence KPI in the executive dashboard of the business.

CUSTOMER LOYALTY

The previous section focused on Customer Service Excellence. Understanding why customer service excellence is important relies on understanding the 'Value Exchange Model.'

The Value Exchange Model relies on four interrelated

The Value Exchange Model

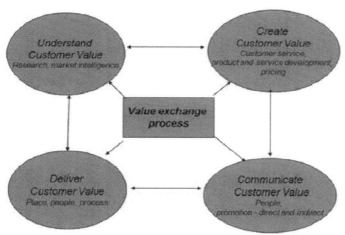

values:

- Understanding Customer Value.

- Creating Customer Value.

- Communicating Customer Value.

- Delivering Customer Value.

> **"...is a difference between a repeat purchase customer and one that is loyal. The difference is commitment."**

Of all the benchmarks used to measure quality, customer satisfaction is still one of the single strongest predictors of customer retention. It's considerably more expensive to attract new customers than it is to keep old ones happy. In a climate of decreasing brand loyalties, understanding customer service and measuring customer satisfaction are crucial. We need to know what expectations customers have of our services and products, the effectiveness of our marketing strategies, the strength of our company's image, as well as the key elements that most heavily influence customer retention for our business. Or, put diagrammatically:

Defining Customer Value

Product value
Service value
Personnel value
Image value

Total customer value

Customer delivered value

Financial cost
Time cost
Energy cost
Psychological cost

Total customer cost

Customer Value is linked to customer loyalty in that there is a difference between a repeat purchase customer and one that is loyal. The difference is commitment. Customer service result is sustainable revenue because it leads to customer loyalty, rather than just repeat purchases, and Customer Value relies on customer service.

The difference in behavior of a loyal customer compared to a repeat purchase customer includes:

- A committed, loyal customer is likely to be more tolerant of mistakes and to see the benefits of a long term relationship with the organization.
- A repeat purchase customer is likely to change organizations when a better offer is made from a competitor.
- Long term customers are a vital source of profitability because:
- They purchase more because they trust you.
- You get to know them and can service their needs more efficiently – and cheaply.
- They provide free advertising through word of mouth.
- As well as the above, attracting new customer's costs money.
- This is through such things as:
- Advertising costs.
- Set up costs for new accounts.
- Learning the customer's requirements.
- Each year that the customer stays amortizes these costs over a longer period of time.
- Organizations with loyal, long term customers can outperform companies with lower unit costs and higher

market share but with a higher customer churn. For example, a 10% reduction in unit costs may be financially equivalent to a 2% decrease in the customer defection rate. Low defection strategies can outperform low cost strategies because most businesses have a defection rate of between 10-20%.

• So how can customer defects be reduced? Some practices to tackle this include:

• a) Watch the door.

• Track customer purchases over time, noting changes in behavior in the total order or the product mix purchased.

• b) Know what defectors are telling you.

• Customers who leave can provide a view of the business that is not available to those on the 'inside'. Unlike market research about customer satisfaction levels, feedback from defecting customers tends to be concrete and specific. Customers are usually able to articulate their reasons and skilful probing can get to their base concerns. It can also highlight areas where improvements will increase customer retention and help decide where investments in improvements are likely to show the greatest return.

• c) Know the cost of acquiring new accounts.

• All staff should be aware of the real costs of acquiring new customers and financial statements should show these costs clearly.

• d) Crafting a zero defections strategy requires an organization to teach all employees:

• The lifetime value of a customer.

• How to gather information, who to share it with and what actions to take.

- A zero defection strategy also applies to staff defections.
- e) Other Considerations.
- The Service Value Chain also requires organizations to recognize that there are internal as well as external customers and that external and internal customer service is dependent on employee retention and employee productivity and that low employee turnover is closely linked to high customer satisfaction.
- In summary then, Best in Class customer service begins with the customer- measuring performance against their expectations. The supply chain functions in any business are pivotal in delivering to expectations and this can be done in conjunction with an 'all of business' approach that uses a Perfect or Error Free Order measurement system. There is a difference though between customer service excellence and customer loyalty. Measuring customer loyalty will be the subject of a future discussion but, finally, here are some keys to great customer service:
- In the eyes of the customer you are the organisation.
- Remember your own experiences as a customer.
- Behave as if they are your only customer.
- Give customers a way to back down without losing face.
- Remember that it is often the little things that are the difference between competitors.
- Take responsibility for the actions of the company.
- Check that what you are doing is what customers want you to do.

- Good customer service results from continual improvement not sporadic redefinitions of business priorities.
- Remember that customers don't know (or care) what your customer satisfaction rating is – only how you react to them today.

CHAPTER 3. UNDERSTANDING THE CRITICAL BOOKENDS

The supply chain network is a critical dimension of the supply chain. As a major component at the operational level, it has a significant impact on overall profitability for the organization concerned. Getting the supply chain network design right can yield improvements in areas such as:

- **Customer allocations to supply points**

- **Sales territory planning**

- **Sourcing strategies**

The design has to be driven by the strategic imperatives of the supply chain, which are in turn linked back to the business objectives of the company.At the same time, it must allow for optimization of the Cost To Serve the end customers. This applies to both new and existing networks. A simplified model that is often useful to keep in mind is that of two bookends to the supply chain network: at one end there is the customer or market to be served; and at the other end is the supplier.

Focusing on network design may also be motivated by signs of any of the following problems:

1. Too many stock locations

2. Poor Distribution Centre utilization

3. Multiple handling

4. High distribution costs

5. Poor customer service

6. Excessive co-location of offices and warehouses

It's important to make sure that the overall design objective is the best one. For instance, businesses sometimes turn to the design or the selection of the location of a new Distribution Center, because of existing facilities reaching capacity. However, there is a whole range of measures and changes that can be adopted within the supply chain to reduce requirements for, or make better use of, DC capacity. In this case, adding more facilities to the network is not necessarily the best solution.

Modeling the Supply Chain Network

Before a network design in particular is implemented, modeling is done to understand the potential advantages or impacts of putting new parts of a network in place. Network modeling can be used to asses a broad range of future alternatives. It's important at the early stages of considering a network modeling project, to clearly articulate and agree the key modeling outcomes required, in terms of what they are and also in terms of their breadth and depth.

These outcomes are often best expressed as "what questions do we want to answer?" or "what different possibilities do we want to test?" Different scenarios that can be explored include:

• Distribution centers (DCs). Number, size and location

• Service levels. Impact of changes

• Transport. Changes to vehicle types or rates

• Customers. Changes to demand

• Customers. Sales territory allocations

• Supply. Impact of changes to supply points and supply volumes

Network modeling can be conducted at different levels of detail depending on the need. A modeling project typically follows these broad stages

1. Scenario Concepts

• Develop preferred and logical future scenarios

• Agree what is constrained and unconstrained

• Also agree on clean sheet scenario approach

2. Base Case Model

• Provides a baseline for comparison of options.

• Provides important cost functions for the modeling.

• Gives insights in the performance of the "As Is" network

3. Scenario Models

• Run agreed scenario models.

• Review results.

• Re run models as required.

• Run sub scenarios based on results.

• Review outcomes.

4. Business Case

• Agree best scenario.

• Develop scenario into comprehensive business case.

• Costs, benefits, risks,

For a viable model and output from the process that truly benefits the business, stakeholder engagement and review at critical stages is vital.

5. Variables and information required

A broad range of variables can be tested within a network modeling approach:

Customers: Location, Volume ordered,

Service needs

Domestic Transport: Mode, Carrier type, Carrier rates,
Service levels

Secondary (Local) Storage: Location, Storage type,

SKUs stored, Volume stored,

Capital costs, Operating costs, Maintenance

Domestic Transport: Mode, Carrier type, Carrier rates,
Service levels

Primary Storage: Location, Storage Type,

SKUs stored, Volume stored,

Capital costs, Operating costs,

Maintenance

Domestic Transport: Mode, Carrier type, Carrier

Rates, Service levels

Port of Entry: Location, Volumes, Process,

Transport Mode, Costs

Supplier/Plants: Location, Volumes, Process,

Transport Mode, Lead Times,

Availability, Performance

Overall: Flow of Products and Services,

Flow of Information and Cash,

Performance and KPIs (Key

Performance Indicators)

Typical information requirements are based on the list below, which shows how different information components generate different master data files. Some components appear in more than one master. If any of this data is not available, alternative approaches can be developed.

Customer Master: Code, description and location details including geo-coding,

Demand History

Material Master: Demand History, Inter Facility

Transfers, Supply History

Facility Master: Transport Rate Cards, Staffing

Levels, Operating Costs,

Material Handling Equipment,

Demand History, Inventory Snapshot Code, description, and location details including geo-coding

Supplier Master: Supply History, Code,

Description and location details including geo-coding.

Assembling this information provides a baseline for the comparison of options and also provides important cost functions for the network modeling. This in turn gives insights into the performance of the existing network.

6. Generating solutions

Solutions can be developed as a logical process based on modeling skills, and sound business and industry experience.

Stakeholder engagement and review at critical stages is vital.

1. Customer base analysis

• Where they are

• What they use (demand)

• Specific constraints/needs

2. Understand the Service offer

• Service needs

• Service performance

• Service costs

These parameters form a key driver of the overall 'shape' and size of the network. They correspond to the first 'bookend' (the customer base).

3. Supplier base analysis

• Where they are

• What they supply

• Specific constraints/needs

4. Understand supplier lead times

• Service performance

• Service and cost trade offs

• Freight terms

Sections 3 and 4 in this list form the 2nd bookend (the supplier base). This drives inbound costs and operating principle such as storage requirements and cross docking.

5. Solution options development

• Known options

• Logical options

• Intuitive options

• Experiential options

From this, conceptual network options are developed and discussed.

6. Model the solutions

• Against a known base case

• Sensitivity analysis

• Additional what if sub-options

A quantitative assessment is made for each option.

7. Challenge and refine the solutions

• Pressure test the options

• Refine the options

Company teams need to challenge and review the options. A preferred option is then selected and a comprehensive business case is built.

Network Modeling Tools

Specialist optimization tools are often preferable as it provides a good audit trail, a sound structure to work within and advanced optimization algorithms.

A tool like this is typically a software application that:

• Tests many different distribution strategies in a relatively short time.

• Provide detailed performance and cost reporting on each option.

• Provide powerful information on customer location and market segmentation.

It takes account of many variables such as:

• **Service levels**

• **Customer profitability**

• **Stock sourcing from suppliers**

• Distribution center location

• **Centralized compared to decentralized stock holding**

• **Facility Rationalization**

• **Modes of transport.**

The full spectrum of supply chain dimensions can be modeled, including for example sample vehicle and depot properties. The supply chain model from this should then accurately represent the costs of moving material through the supply chain to allow option and sensitivity modeling.

Early base model outputs include the mapping of the demand density. This gives valuable insights into demand from a geographic perspective. Further 'drill downs' by division, customer group or product group will give further detailed interpretation. Often poor customer/supply allocations show up here.

Base case model costs are calibrated to within two to five per cent of actual costs so that future scenario models accurately represent likely costs. Base model outputs also give a clear view of how product is currently flowing through the network.

Scenario Modeling

Following Base Model calibration, a broad range of scenarios can then be run to test change in supply points, DCs, customer service, transport type and the like.

Again, all models are supported by detailed analysis of cost and service. To categories them in detail, costs are first broken down into broad categories such as:

• Warehousing fixed & Variable

• Inbound freight

• Outbound freight

Network design trade-offs

Within the different options available, the choice of the "best" one may simply be a matter of deciding which tradeoff is the most acceptable. For example, more stocking points typically means more cubic meters of storage underroof. Some of the implications of this for a company may be:

• Higher lease or facility rental costs

• Greater complexity in operational management

• Being closer to the customer for faster service

• Replenishment can become more onerous

Trade-offs as the number of inventory points in a network increases are typically between the following:

• The cost of storage rises, due to the increase in facility numbers and fixed costs

• Inventory holding cost (cost of capital) increases as more inventory is required (due to increased safety stock requirements with more locations)

• Primary transport, or line haul cost increases, as more tonnes/kms are being travelled

• Customer delivery cost (secondary transport) decreases, as with more facilities, the distance to the customer reduces

• DC systems costs increase, as more licenses, interfaces and hardware may be required.

Inventory holding costs can increase significantly as additional nodes are added into a network. A possible alternative for a company may be to pool inventory in fewer locations thereby lowering the total system inventory. As nodes are changed, the company may also need to pay particular attention to slow moving or obsolete stock to ensure that if they continue to be held, it's part of a deliberate, thought-out plan to do so. The extent to which a company can engage suppliers to deliver directly to line stations or DC's may be an important consideration.

While service levels can be significantly increased by adding stocking points, the company must ensure that a balance is struck so that they are not 'over servicing' their customer base and adding in unnecessary costs. The right systems capabilities can make a significant difference to overall supply chain performance.

Moving towards design optimization

Optimization of a supply chain network can differ considerably according to the business concerned. However, the underlying principle is always to pick the lowest total cost points. It's also critical that the network supports the company's overall supply chain strategy.

The secret to an efficient distribution network is to minimize the amount of product handling. It's a good exercise for any company to think about its own distribution networks and to try to count the number of touches a product receives between the point of supply and the customer. Each touch not only incurs cost, but also increases the risk of error and damage.

The objective within any distribution network is to find the optimum number of facilities that will reduce the total cost curve, whilst still maintaining appropriate levels of customer service. We need to understand what drives, or should drive businesses to select certain locations over others. In fact, the cost driver that frequently has the least impact on the total cost of selecting a given location is land and building cost. This is due to the fact that inbound and outbound transport, as well as labor costs are a far higher proportion of the total costs of a distribution network.

The customer base and the service offer provided to customers have a direct bearing on where a company needs to hold stock to service them. Likewise, the location of the company's suppliers has a similar impact. The further away the supplier base, and the more unreliable the supplier service, so the more stock needs to held in the network to ensure service continuity. The signs of a problem in a supply chain network are many, but not always obvious. For example, many businesses co-locate sales branches with warehouses. This is rarely necessary and may just lead to a network with too many branches, too much stock and high distribution costs.

A company needs to look for multiple paths from source to customer. It's important to understand that the traditional path, through a company's own stock holding facilities might not always be the most effective from a cost and service perspective. For example, direct delivery from supplier to customer can be appropriate where the lead times, order size and transport efficiency make sense – the fewer times a product is touched through the supply chain, the less cost is incurred.

Examples of supply chain improvements through network design

A company in Thailand was distributing products nationally using a large network of warehouses to service customers in up country areas. The customers were ordering in small quantities and the distribution costs were very high with many orders being expedited at a high cost directly from Bangkok. A simple change to the network involved closing the up country warehouses and using distributors in these areas. Products were then shipped up country in bulk, by the truck load and the distributors serviced the small local customers.The price reduction to the distributors was more than offset by the reduced transport and warehouse costs. The new network operated well, savings were higher than forecasted and sales increased as well.

An FMCG company in Australia had grown over time to have a network of over 40 warehouses. This number was thought to be required to provide a high level of service to customers. In fact with careful network modeling using specialist tools, it was possible to prove that a network of 20 warehouses located in the appropriate locations could offer just as high service levels but with much lower operating and inventory costs. That network operated as expected after this rationalization and the cost savings were significant.

CHAPTER 4. PROLOGUE

"Come on! Get out from behind your desk! Leave your e-mails – they can wait! Let's go for a wander through your warehouse. I know you'd like to do this more often, but there always seems to be something that crops up to keep you tied to your desk. Customer complaints, supplier problems, demands for budget information from Finance, inventory inaccuracy, labor problems, lack of storage space, a proposed visit from City analysts hosted by the CEO are all conspiring to keep you from doing what you are paid to do: managing your warehouse most effectively and efficiently.

"OK, here we are in the receiving bay. Every dock has a vehicle either being unloaded, waiting for someone to start the processor to complete the paperwork. Look outside, over to the gatehouse, and you can see there is a queue of trucks waiting to come into the yard, but they can't enter because the vehicle waiting area is choc-full. This happens every day, about this time, but is usually clear by half-way through the evening shift.

"On the floor in the receiving area, wall-to-wall pallets are waiting to be put to bed. The fork-lift operators are having a problem identifying and collecting their next load

Because of the clutter.This is slowing them down, and the backlog is building. What's that? You have put in a request for another two forklifts to cope with the peak put-away, but it has been turned down by those cretins in Finance? Mmmm…. well, let's look at that later.

"Let's take a walk through the pallet storage area. Looking up and along the line of the racking, we can see the occasional badly located pallet protruding out from the

beam. The pallet is being supported, not by the corner block as intended, but by the weaker stringer boards. This is a safety issue; a weak or cracked stringer is in danger of giving way, and a pallet load of product falling from the fifth level of racking can easily ruin someone's entire day.
"There are pallets of stock in the aisles waiting to be located, either in storage locations or a ground level pickface location. Look at that forklift operator trying to access an upper-level location to perform a full-pallet pick for an urgent order. She has had to move that obstructing pallet on the ground to make the play.

"We are now near the end of an aisle nearest the marshaling area.These are the prime pick-face locations where picking activity should be at its highest.Hang on; this full pallet of stock appears to have a thick layer of dust on its stretch-wrapped surface.It hasn't been picked from for a very long time.I've been watching that picker just over there. He is using a fork lift rather than a ground level order picker to drop the pallet from the upper levels, pick the cases and then replace the pallet. Why is he doing that? Shouldn't that fork lift be operating in the receiving area to tackle the put-away backlog?
"Over in the corner, on the floor against the wall, is about twenty or thirty pallets holding a collection of some three hundred or so items in varying conditional states. Around this collection of apparent misfits is a cordon formed by tape, not unlike that used by the police to cordon off a crime scene. Perhaps this is an apt simile because there are handwritten placards warning passers-by: 'Not on account – do not inventory'!

"How is the order picking going? All today's orders have been picked apart from a few that need to be completed because there was no stock in the pick face location at the time of picking. It was a light day for orders, was it?

Where have all the pickers disappeared to?
"Now we cross to the marshaling area where the loads are being assembled in order of drop and checked before being loaded. With all the orders picked, the floor is full – covered in pallets and roll cages waiting to be processed for dispatch when the vehicles eventually arrive. Because of the overcrowding, the demarcation spaces between loads have all but disappeared, and there is a danger of stock migrating from one checked load to another.

"OK, I have a good idea of what is going on. Let's head back to the office. By the way, I didn't see your supervisors on the floor. Ah, there they are: in the supervisors' office, working through their e-mails!"

These vignettes are taken from reality. I have seen them all several times as a consultant and as a DC manager, singly and in multiples. They are all symptoms of a malaise that might originate in the warehouse, but equally might be due to external causes.

TREAT THE SYMPTOMS OR ATTACK THE DISEASE?
Most mothers instinctively know about symptoms and their relationship with cause. The first thing a mother will do if a child complains of feeling unwell is to feel their forehead. If she feels a high temperature, she knows it indicates a problem elsewhere – it is highly unlikely that the heat source is on the surface of the forehead – and will start searching for the reason. If there are no other obvious symptoms she

might leave it overnight, ease the discomfort of the patient with a cooling towel or proprietary medicine and wait to see what develops. If there is no improvement, or more significant signs emerge, such as a rash, she will then seek the help of a professional in the form of a doctor.

A warehouse is a place where many of the symptoms of a problematic supply chain come to the surface. You could say it is the forehead of the supply chain. The causes may well come from within the facility or its operation, but quite often they are rooted elsewhere. The "Complete Warehouse Manager" gets into the habit of looking for the indicators on a daily basis, tackling the immediate effects of the symptom, but then delving deeper to find and rectify the cause. In a large operation, the supervisors should take on the role of "Mother" looking for and reducing the impact of the symptoms, and report to the Warehouse Manager/"Doctor" to follow up with a deeper diagnosis. If the Doctor can't follow the trail to and rectify the cause, then he will refer the case to a "Specialist" also known as – surprise – a Consultant!

CASE STUDY – TIME TRAVELLING LOGISTICS!
A classic case of trying to cure a disease by treating symptoms only, instead of tackling the cause, was to be found when I arrived in Thailand as the newly-appointed Group Logistics Director of an international trading group whose Thailand operation, at the time, had about four warehouses in and around Bangkok and seven transshipment facilities scattered throughout the country. The flagship distribution center had only just been completed and commissioned six months earlier. The aim

was to close down the smaller warehouses and consolidate their operations into the new Central DC. This should have already happened, but the commissioning of the new facility had not gone well. The operation was, in effect, falling over. The Thai General Manager of the facility had suffered a nervous breakdown and moved elsewhere, so I was doing his job as well.

The DC had a 3PL (3rd Party Logistics) role mostly for internal Group Business Units (BU) and some external customers. The biggest complaint was that target dates for delivery to the end-user customers were being missed by as much as seven days or more for about 65% of the orders received. The proof was in the computer-generated reports, which the Managing Director of one of the BUs showed me with great alacrity at the Group Operational Board Meeting held on my second day in the post.

The report he showed me was a Tunguska Report, named after the region of Siberia where a meteoroid or comet exploded in 1908, devastating 2,150 square kilometers of virgin forest. Producing it must have had the same impact on the environment. It covered every order going back to the first day of operation six months ago and indeed showed that the majority of target dates had been missed. I had the slightly intuitive feeling that he was trying to make a point, or I was being set up – or both.

A review of a report subsequently pulled from the WMS showed that the vast majority of the errant orders were passed through to the DC after the target date had passed. Investigation showed that orders were often put on hold by the sales staff for customer credit checks, lack of stock to meet the order or other administrative reasons – some valid, some not so valid and some downright nefarious. However, the target date was not amended to reflect the delay. In other words, in many cases, the target dates were missed even before the DC received the order. H.G. Wells!

Where are you when I need your time machine?
The effect on what should have been the successful operation of this brand new, multi-million dollar investment was devastating. Management and staff were trying, as a priority, to fulfill orders that were the subject of outraged customer complaints and at the same time meet the new orders that were coming down the pipeline every day. The small fires of the crisis were joining together and turning into a conflagration that was being fought with little buckets of water, albeit with considerable honest endeavor and personal sacrifice on the part of the DC staff, particularly on the part of the General Manager.

The solution? Ensure that the target date was amended on the sales system to incorporate any delay in the sales process. All outstanding orders that had been recorded as missed were canceled and resubmitted if they were still valid and required by the customer. A wall-to-wall, blind stock count was held to set a baseline of accurate stock levels which had also been in chaos for six months. In other words, the rain stopped play in the first over with no runs scored.the C'mon boys, let's start the game again!

Within two months, the DC was delivering 85% of its orders nationwide within 24 hours and 98% within 48 hours, against a target for all orders of 95% within 48 hours of the order being passed to the DC. Just as importantly, the cost of overtime was slashed by 90%. This had been running at the same level as, or greater than, salaries for normal operations.

This improvement was not all down to the target date issue, but the reduction in pressure about missed delivery target dates in the system meant that the management team could then spend time looking into and solving the other issues that typically plague a newly commissioned logistics facility.

SYMPTOMS OR CAUSES?
In the same way that a cardiologist has not only detailed knowledge of the heart but also has excellent knowledge of the rest of the body systems, so should warehouse managers have a good working knowledge of the other elements of the supply chain they are supporting as well as an intimate knowledge of their operations? This will enable them to conduct relevant self- criticism, while at the same time looking upstream and downstream for the other possible causes of their problems. Sometimes a single symptom might be generated concurrently by internal and external issues.
Let's take a look at the examples in the Prologue and perform a diagnosis of the possible causes.

Firstly, the chaos in the yard and the receiving bay could be caused by:
•   No booking in system for deliveries, or if there is, it is not being adhered to. If deliveries are booked in and controlled,

the workload is spread evenly across the normal shift allowing resources to be optimised.

Overtime can then be used for genuine problems.
•   Some companies allow suppliers to make their delivery schedules, leaving the warehouse to cope with the resultant chaos in the yard and in the receiving bay itself. I believe the sales department should allocate the week in arrangement with the supplier; the warehouse should set the day and time within that week.

Wall-to-wall pallets in the receiving area waiting for putting away:
•   This could be a direct result of the lack of control of deliveries as described above. Also, to what degree are the quality checks were conducted and are they necessary?
A system of vendor rating linked with the level of QC relevant to that rating could speed up the putting away of stock. Remember, the stock is generally not available for issue until it has been put into the location.

•   There might be an FLT (Fork Lift Truck) resource issue, but increasing the number should be very much the last resort and only if a full check of the fleet utilization has been conducted. If a truck is being used for case-level order picking, as observed in our Prologue, then it is being used to cover an inefficient pick face layout at the expense of putting stock away.

The location of pallets on racking is a good indicator of two issues:

- How skillful your FLT operators are and whether they have a pride in their performance and how effective your supervisors are. Are they too busy fighting fires to check on safety and housekeeping issues, or do they have a poor attitude to the leadership and discipline required to run a high-quality warehouse operation?

Pick faces should be considered dynamic and not static. If the dead or slow-moving stock is in a prime pick-face location, then the whole pick trail should be reviewed. Dust on the stock is a great yardstick that indicates the popularity – or lack of it – of stock. If too many examples are found, then dive in deeper with stock movement reports.

Items not on the account should not be tolerated in a warehouse, except under extreme circumstances. Everything should be accounted for in some way and consequently liable for stock count action. The product designated as not to be inventoried promoting and encouraging fraud and theft.

The absence of pickers working on the shop floor or the completion of the pick workload too early in the day suggests that the picking teams are not being managed. Preplanning the pick and allocating the right number of pickers to complete the pick requirement in line with the dispatch schedule within the shift times will release resources to carry out the numerous other tasks that are forgotten about when the pressure is on, such as housekeeping, stock counts, stock relocation and pick face maintenance.

This is also linked to how orders are released for picking. Order release should be linked to the time to process the order, which should be linked to the departure time, linked in turn to the traveling time finally linked to the delivery time. Work backward down that chain and group the orders together that need to be dispatched together from the warehouse. Orders should not be sitting on the despatch bay floor for hours on end. Think of how you plan a journey by rail or air. You start with when and where you want to arrive at your destination and work back from there. So should it be with planning the picking operation?

Above all, get your supervisors away from their computers and onto the shop floor doing what they should be doing: supervising and looking for symptoms!

CHAPTER 5. TRANSPORT – THE FOUR BIGGEST MISTAKES BUSINESSES MAKE WHEN BUYING TRANSPORT SERVICES.

What makes these mistakes the biggest? The fact that they are so fundamentally got wrong!

Would you commit to paying thousands of dollars for a suit without knowing what size it was? Would you drive aimlessly around town looking for a tailor to make it? Would you stop at every repair and alteration shop you saw, just in case they could do the job? When you happened to find a tailor, would you leave the fabric choice up to him? When he gave you the bill, would you accept the proposition that, if you can't make a suit and didn't see the tailor make it, you have little hope of understanding why it costs what it does?

No? Then why, every day, do companies buying transport services make the same mistakes of:

1. Not understanding the needs of their customers.

2. Not having an effective tendering strategy.

3. Not talking with the right companies.

4. Not understanding the cost drivers.

In this chapter, we'll examine why and also see how, in most instances, the mistakes can be easily avoided.

One: Not Understanding What Your Customer Needs

Where distribution is concerned, it's often the case that companies look at their customers as a single group with an individual service requirement. Of course there are always the few squeaky wheels whose demands are accommodated, but in general, the result is an undifferentiated service standard.

It is also often the case that companies set their service standards, not by what they know their customers need, but by what their competitors are doing. This is particularly prevalent in time-critical industries. There is a presumption that the service standard that evolves from competitors trying to "out-service" each other is driven by the industry they supply. In fact, companies are responding to a perceived competitive advantage and not their customers, some of whom may end up being over-serviced.

Companies that adopt either of these approaches to set service standards are spending too much and not necessarily satisfying their customers.

> **"Realising that your customers don't all share the same characteristics and needs, then identifying the differences, can save you money."**

Realising that your customers don't all share the same characteristics and needs, then identifying the differences, can save you money. Even within highly time-sensitive industries, such as spare parts and medical equipment distribution, there are differences in service requirements.

A few simple examples illustrate this:

1. In the healthcare field, expensive "on loan" medical devices need to be flown to interstate hospitals on a "next flight" basis. However, the inexpensive consumables that the devices use can be sent to the central store of the hospital by road. Both services satisfy the customer's needs.

2. In the distribution of spare parts, orders can be designated according to their level of urgency, allowing a consolidation of non-urgent or replenishment orders to be transported on a cheaper and slower basis. Again, both services satisfy the customer's needs.

Typically, companies that have a poor understanding of their customers' needs have another failing in common; either they don't have a business strategy that encompasses their supply chain, or their supply chain strategy is misaligned. In the context of understanding customer needs, the most pertinent point to make is that with a properly aligned supply chain strategy, customer needs would be well-profiled.

This doesn't mean that you can't get better alignment between customer needs and service standards unless you develop a supply chain strategy. You simply need to recognise that customers are not all the same and that neither are your products. Translate this into the context of your distribution service standards and you will save money.

Two: Not Having an Effective Tendering Strategy

Many companies have poor strategies for engaging the carrier market; some have none at all. This situation often arises from a reluctance to develop a strategy, based on the misconception that a detailed knowledge of the carrier market is required. Without a strategy, Distribution or Transport Managers will typically:

1. Appoint too many carriers, breaking up the work and losing the potential for price leveraging.

2. Find themselves forced to award some work on the basis that there's only one option in the mix.

3. Create a larger than necessary administrative and performance management task.

4. Create a larger than necessary range of service cultures.

No matter how large or small your company's distribution spend, having a strategy for engaging the market will achieve three things: it will allow you to leverage better rates, it will simplify dealings with carriers and it will promote consistency of service.

> "No matter how large or small your company's distribution spend, having a strategy for engaging the market will achieve three things: it will allow you to leverage better rates, it will simplify dealings with carriers and it will promote consistency of service."

By applying three key principles, you can develop an effective strategy regardless of your knowledge of the market players. At this stage, you're only interested in how you approach the market, not who you approach.

The key principals are:

1. Aim for the smallest field of tenderers necessary to meet your service goals.

2. Always provide yourself with several options for each segment of work.

3. Bundle the work into the largest possible segments.

The first two principles rely on getting the right combination of reach and service mix. In this regard, carriers can be characterised as:

• **Having a broad range of service offerings.**

• **Having a national footprint.**

• **Being a service specialist.**

• **Being a regional specialist.**

By including a small number of companies that have the first two characteristics, you can minimise the need to include companies that have the latter two, while maintaining multiple options. An example of this would be to include a national carrier that has local distribution capability in every capital city, as well as a specialist local distribution company for each capital.

The result of successfully applying these two principles is to optimise your ability to effectively manage service performance by reducing the contact points. The effect of the third principle is to maximise your ability to achieve the best available rates through volume leveraging. When bundling the work, it is also necessary to ensure each segment is commercially viable. This will allow you to award standalone segments if necessary, while still being able to leverage the remainder to best effect.

Three: Talking with the Wrong Companies

One of the easiest mistakes to make when buying transport services is to engage with the wrong companies, often accompanied by the mistake of talking with too many companies. This can be enormously time-consuming, frustrating, costly and damaging to your company's reputation. It will expose you to poor choices that will disrupt your distribution services and almost inevitably lead you to repeat the process within one to two years, firmly believing it was the carrier's fault.

> **"One of the easiest mistakes to make when buying transport services is to engage with the wrong companies, often accompanied by the mistake of talking with too many companies."**

Talking with the wrong or too many companies can have negative repercussions, even with those carriers that aren't awarded work. You will almost certainly have a substantial over-run with your tendering timetable, due to underestimating the lengthy evaluation process required. You will also struggle to manage communication of the process in a professional way. Perhaps most importantly, you will be labelled as ignorant of the market when many of the invited tenderers realise they are a poor match for your service requirements and that you have wasted their time.

Engaging with the wrong people can result from quite divergent approaches. You may have wanted to limit yourself to what you're familiar with. This seems reasonable, but may simply confirm that your experience of the market is too narrow.

Have you addressed the issue of who to invite into a tender using one or both of the following tactics:

1. Automatically including all of the incumbent carriers.

2. Automatically including the tier one, national brands.

3. If you have, you're sticking to your comfort zone.

Alternately, you may have wanted to "cast a wide net". Accordingly, you may have applied the above tactics, as well as one or several of the following:

1. Dragged out all the business cards and rate offers from carriers who have knocked on your door in the past few years.

2. Canvassed colleagues, competitors and friends about who they use for transport.

3. Trawled the Internet by geographic region.

4. In very few circumstances would this have been a sound approach, more often than not it would simply have meant that you were being indiscriminate.

The most effective way to avoid the mistake of engaging the wrong companies is to build a basic understanding of the carrier market. This can be done with little effort, when you consider it's simply a matter of accumulating information in an effective way.

There are three elements to building an understanding of the market that will allow you to target the most suitable carriers when the need arises. These are:

1. Develop a service specification and capability statement.

This is the most time-consuming, but also the most critical element. The service specification will tell a prospective carrier enough about your products, network, customers and distribution needs to be able to complete a specified capability statement.

2. Issue the service specification and capability statement to carriers.

Once you have developed the documents, you will be more attuned to the compatibility between your company and carriers that come knocking. Those that pass scrutiny as well as those that you have identified through research should receive the documents.

Evaluate the capability statements and identify the pre-qualified companies.

By pre-qualifying carriers in this way, you can establish a smaller field of tenderers, all of which can meet your service standards. Pre-qualification may also help with confirming the quality and availability of certain carrier types in the market. This will be useful in determining your strategy for going to tender.

> **"Having a basic understanding of your carriers' cost drivers will allow you to negotiate better rates and modify your distribution operations to reduce transport costs. Many companies lack this understanding."**

Four: Not Understanding the Cost Drivers

Having a basic understanding of your carriers' cost drivers will allow you to negotiate better rates and modify your distribution operations to reduce transport costs. Many companies lack this understanding.

The simple reason for this is that, historically, carriers have closely guarded this information. In the past, carriers almost universally held the view that the benefits of greater operational efficiency, engineering improvements and other technological improvements to their businesses were theirs' alone. This has meant that they were reluctant to discuss their operations in terms of cost drivers and what they saw as competitive advantage.

This is no longer the prevailing view, although many carriers are still not proactive in discussing ways to help their customers save money.It's also the case that many transport service users are not aware of this shift in attitude. Consequently, there are Distribution Managers that still refrain from asking what goes on once the truck pulls away from the back door and who lack an understanding of how they can influence this.

This lack of understanding is potentially costing them money in two ways.Firstly, they may accept a more expensive and inappropriate rate structure. The following examples illustrate this.

1. A company distributing FMCG products despatches pallets of varying heights that will bear double-stacking. On average, the pallets are less than 1.0 metre high. The

Distribution Manager negotiates a pallet rate with his carrier, which entails his company paying for the entire space, from floor to ceiling. If he understood that the carrier's aim was to return a yield for every pallet space and also understood the physical dimensions of the space, he could negotiate to standardise his pallets to 0.8 meters high and be charged a half pallet rate. The carrier could then charge either the same customer or another for use of the other half pallet space. If he did not understand this dynamic, he would be paying to transport air!

2. A company distributing food products despatches pallets of varying heights above 1.5 metres that will bear double-stacking. The Distribution Manager has two quotes; one a pallet rate from a pallet specialist and the other a per kilogram rate from a bulk and loose freight consolidator. If the Distribution Manager understood the load characteristics of each carrier's operation, he would realise that the consolidator could improve his yield for the pallet space on offer with someone else's loose freight, whereas, because of the height constraint, the pallet specialist could not double stack. Assuming both carriers were trying to achieve the same yield per pallet space, the kilogram rate will always be the most cost-effective. The wrong rate choice through a failure to understand this dynamic will result in a significant cost penalty. It will also expose the service user to greater cost inefficiency if the average weight per pallet decreases.

Having a poor understanding of the carriers' cost drivers can also impact through the service user's distribution practices. In this case, there is the potential for saving rather than the potential for greater cost. This is illustrated by the following example.

A manufacturer uses road freight services to supply its customers nationally. The freight for all states except Western Australia is ready for despatch by 2:00pm. Due to the time difference, order close-off for Western Australia is two hours later and the freight is ready for despatch at 4:00pm. All of the freight is picked up in the same vehicle at 4:30pm.

What the Distribution Manager is unaware of, and the carrier has not been proactive in discussing, is that it would reduce the carrier's costs by getting its line-haul away earlier if more freight could be sorted earlier in the day. If the Distribution Manager was aware of this, he could arrange a 2:00pm despatch and negotiate a rate reduction for the relevant freight. If he is unaware of this fact, he is effectively paying for his freight to sit in his warehouse.

By understanding a few basic dynamics you will be able to identify opportunities that will reduce your costs:

1. **Carriers quote their rates in a range of charge units to standardise the revenue yield per load. The aim is for you to pay for any empty space.**

   The best charge unit is the one that most closely equates to reality. Rates for pallets, skids and cartons are based on nominal dimensions – you pay the same regardless of variations in actual dimensions. Kilogram rates are based on a physical fact – you pay for what you use.

2. **The more a carrier can contract its depot operating time, the lower its costs.**

   If you can take advantage of under-utilised freight handlers during the early afternoon, you will contribute to the line-haul vehicles departing sooner and the depot closing earlier. You should negotiate a rate on this basis.

3. **In the Express Freight market, line-haul revenue yield is driven by the mix of freight density.**

   Very dense freight, when correctly blended with less dense freight, can significantly increase revenue yield. As freight of this type is attractive to carriers, but far less common than lighter, bulkier freight, rates can be negotiated at a discount.

OTHER BOOKS BY ANDREI BESEDIN

50 Most Powerful Excel Functions and Formulas: Advanced Ways to Save Your Time and Make Complex Analysis Quick and Easy!

https://www.amazon.com/Most-Powerful-Excel-Functions-Formulas/dp/1521549915/ref=zg_bs_1 32559011_7?_encoding=UTF8&psc=1 &refRID=QT5D1NR6CBRAFTGEP7 AG

SECRETS OF LOOKUP: become more productive with lookup, free you're time!

https://www.amazon.com/SECRETS-LOOKUP-PRODUCTIVE-VLOOKUP-Training-ebook/dp/B073P4FVSG/ref=la_B0721 1P1NS_1_10?s=books&ie=UTF8&qid =1499524730&sr=1-10

Top 3 Excel Formulas and Functions https://www.amazon.com/Excel-Formulas-Functions-Training-

Book-
ebook/dp/B0738LF8LL/ref=sr_1_6?ie
=UTF8&qid=1499524945&sr=8-
6&keywords=top+3+excel

Amazing JAVA: Learn JAVA Quickly!

https://www.amazon.com/Amazing-
JAVA-Learn-Quickly-
ebook/dp/B0737762M8/ref=la_B0721
1P1NS_1_2?s=books&ie=UTF8&qid=
1499524891&sr=1-
2&refinements=p_82%3AB07211P1N
S

Dash Diet to Make Middle Aged People Healthy and Fit: 40 Delicious Recipes for People Over 40 Years Old!

https://www.amazon.com/Dash-Diet-Middle-People-Healthy-ebook/dp/B071WZBZPB/ref=la_B072 11P1NS_1_3?s=books&ie=UTF8&qid =1499524891&sr=1-3&refinements=p_82%3AB07211P1N S

Mediterranean diet for middle aged people: 40 delicious recipes to make

people over 40 years old healthy and fit!

https://www.amazon.com/Mediterrane
an-diet-middle-aged-people-
ebook/dp/B0723952FH/ref=la_B0721
1P1NS_1_4?s=books&ie=UTF8&qid=
1499524891&sr=1-
4&refinements=p_82%3AB07211P1N
S

Fitness for Middle Aged People: 40 Powerful Exercises to Make People over 40 Years Old Healthy and Fit!

https://www.amazon.com/Fitness-Middle-Aged-People-Exercises-ebook/dp/B072VFBT99/ref=la_B07211P1NS_1_5?s=books&ie=UTF8&qid=1499524891&sr=1-5&refinements=p_82%3AB07211P1NS

Market Research: Global Market for Germanium and Germanium Products

https://www.amazon.com/Market-Research-Global-Germanium-Products-ebook/dp/B00X4JBM92/ref=la_B0721

1P1NS_1_9?s=books&ie=UTF8&qid=

1499524891&sr=1-

9&refinements=p_82%3AB07211P1N

S

Stocks, Mutual Funds: the Startup Guide on Stock Investing

https://www.amazon.com/Stocks-

Mutual-Funds-Start-Investing-

ebook/dp/B00WOGXCDU/ref=la_B07

211P1NS_1_6?s=books&ie=UTF8&qi

d=1499524891&sr=1-

6&refinements=p_82%3AB07211P1N
S

Aerobics, running & jogging: 30 Minutes a Day Burn Fat Workout for Middle Aged Men"! Two most powerful ways to burn fat quickly!

https://www.amazon.com/Aerobics-running-jogging-Minutes-powerful-ebook/dp/B00WA9ESG6/ref=la_B072
11P1NS_1_7?s=books&ie=UTF8&qid
=1499524891&sr=1-
7&refinements=p_82%3AB07211P1N
S

Diamond Cut Six Packs: How to Develop Fantastic Abs

https://www.amazon.com/Diamond-Cut-Six-Packs-Fantastic-ebook/dp/B01E2OELVS/ref=la_B072 11P1NS_1_8?s=books&ie=UTF8&qid =1499524891&sr=1-8&refinements=p_82%3AB07211P1N S

15 MOST POWERFUL FEATURES OF PIVOT TABLES! Save Your Time with MS Excel!

https://www.amazon.com/MOST-
POWERFUL-FEATURES-PIVOT-
TABLES-
ebook/dp/B074THF418/ref=sr_1_3?ie
=UTF8&qid=1504594835&sr=8-
3&keywords=besedin

**20 Most Powerful Excel Conditional
Formatting Techniques! Save Your
Time with MS Excel**

https://www.amazon.com/Powerful-
Excel-Conditional-Formatting-
Techniques-
ebook/dp/B074H9W6XJ/ref=sr_1_4?i

e=UTF8&qid=1504594835&sr=8-
4&keywords=besedin

Secrets of MS Excel VBA/Macros for Beginners: Save Your Time With Visual Basic Macros!

https://www.amazon.com/Secrets-
Excel-VBA-Macros-Beginners-
ebook/dp/B075GYBLWT/ref=sr_1_7?
ie=UTF8&qid=1506057725&sr=8-
7&keywords=besedin

Secrets of Business Plan Writing: Business Plan Template and Financial Model Included!

https://www.amazon.com/Secrets-Business-Plan-Writing-Financial-ebook/dp/B076GJK8T1/ref=sr_1_9?ie=UTF8&qid=1509858352&sr=8-9&keywords=besedin

Top Numerical Methods with Matlab for Beginners!

https://www.amazon.com/Top-Numerical-Methods-Matlab-Beginners-

ebook/dp/B078HZV7VJ/ref=sr_1_4?ie
=UTF8&qid=1516703667&sr=8-
4&keywords=besedin

**Secrets of Access Database
Development and Programming!**

https://www.amazon.com/Secrets-
Access-Database-Development-
Programming-
ebook/dp/B0776FZVG6/ref=sr_1_3?ie
=UTF8&qid=1516703667&sr=8-
3&keywords=besedin

MS Excel Bible: Save Your Time with MS Excel! 8 Quality Excel Books in 1 Package

https://www.amazon.com/MS-Excel-Bible-Quality-Package-ebook/dp/B077WGQPBN/ref=sr_1_14?ie=UTF8&qid=1516703667&sr=8-14&keywords=besedin

Why Your Body Water Balance Is a Key to Health and Great Shape?

https://www.amazon.com/Water-Balance-Health-Great-Shape-ebook/dp/B0787WCQ4V/ref=sr_1_16

?ie=UTF8&qid=1516703667&sr=8-
16&keywords=besedin

**Top 20 MS Excel VBA Simulations!
VBA to Model Risk, Investments,
Growth, Gambling, and Monte
Carlo Analysis**

https://www.amazon.com/Top-Excel-
VBA-Simulations-Investments-
ebook/dp/B077P52LK7/ref=sr_1_17?i
e=UTF8&qid=1516703944&sr=8-
17&keywords=besedin

Secrets of Building Successful Business Plan for Farm and Rural Business!

https://www.amazon.com/Secrets-Building-Successful-Business-Rural-ebook/dp/B077BZJ3JF/ref=sr_1_20?ie=UTF8&qid=1516703944&sr=8-20&keywords=besedin

Thank You but Can I Ask you for a Favor?

Let me say thank you for downloading and reading my book. This would be all about the training. Hope you enjoyed it but you need to keep on learning to be perfect! If you enjoyed this book, found it useful or otherwise then I'd really grateful it if you would post a short review on Amazon. I read all the reviews personally so I can get your feedback and make this book even better.

Thanks for your support!

Andrei Besedin © 2018

Made in the USA
Middletown, DE
28 April 2021